D1481115

ANIMAL ABC

Pat Stewart

DOVER PUBLICATIONS
Garden City, New York

Copyright

Copyright © 1999 by Pat Stewart
All rights reserved.

Bibliographical Note

Animal ABC is a new work, first published by Dover Publications in 1999.

International Standard Book Number

ISBN-13: 978-0-486-45086-5
ISBN-10: 0-486-45086-4

Manufactured in the United States of America
45086408   2023
www.doverpublications.com

NOTE

Your child will enjoy learning the ABCs by coloring the large letter shapes and animal illustrations in this book. To help your child decipher each letter, ask him or her to use a finger to trace each large letter drawing. It's lots of fun to do together, and it often makes it easier for a beginner to remember the 26 letters of the alphabet.

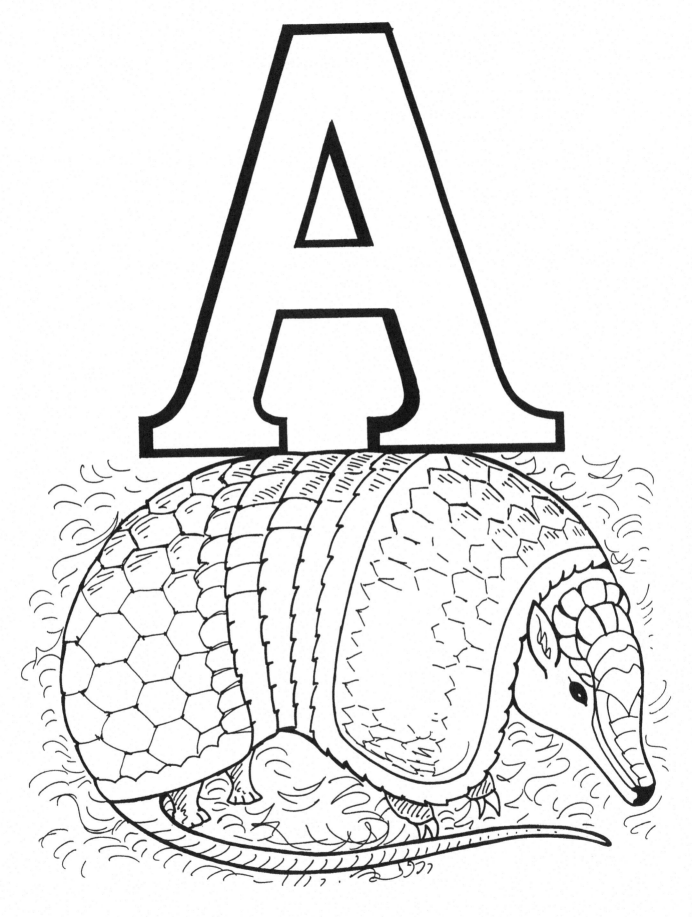

Armadillo

Buffalo

Cow

Deer

Elephant

Frog

Giraffe

Horse

Iguana

Jaguar

Koala

Leopard

Moose

Newt

Octopus

Pig

Quail

Raccoon

Seal

Turkey

Unicorn

Vicuna

Whale

Xiphias

Yak

Zebra

Can you think of other animals whose names begin
with each of the letters of the alphabet?
Write their names in the space next to each letter.

A _____   N _____

B _____   O _____

C _____   P _____

D _____   Q _____

E _____   R _____

F _____   S _____

G _____   T _____

H _____   U _____

I _____   V _____

J _____   W _____

K _____   X _____

L _____   Y _____

M _____   Z _____

Use this page to draw
pictures of your favorite animals.